Diggin Dinosaurs

Curtis Slepian, M.A.

Smithsonian

Contributing Author

Allison Duarte

Consultants

Hans-Dieter Sues, Ph.D.
Paleontologist
National Museum of Natural History

Stephanie Anastasopoulos, M.Ed.
TOSA, STREAM Integration
Solana Beach School District

Publishing Credits

Rachelle Cracchiolo, M.S.Ed., *Publisher*
Conni Medina, M.A.Ed., *Managing Editor*
Diana Kenney, M.A.Ed., NBCT, *Content Director*
Véronique Bos, *Creative Director*
Robin Erickson, *Art Director*
Michelle Jovin, M.A., *Associate Editor*
Mindy Duits, *Senior Graphic Designer*
Smithsonian Science Education Center

Image Credits: front cover, p.1, p.18 (top), p.6, pp.10–11 (all), 12 (bottom), 13 (top), pp.14–15 (all), p.16 (middle left, center and right), p.17 (all), pp.18–19 (all), p.24–25 (all), p.31, p.32 (all) © Smithsonian; pp.2–3 Photomontage/Shutterstock; p.7 Gary Hincks/Science Source; p.9 (bottom left) Lamanna MC, Sues H-D, Schachner ER, Lyson TR [CC 1.0]; p.12 (top right) NG Images/Alamy; p.13 (bottom) Anton Ivanov/Shutterstock; p.20 Phil Velasquez/MCT/Newscom; p.21 Courtesy of The Field Museum, photo by Kate Golembiewski; pp.22–23 (all) Nikki Kahn/The Washington Post via Getty Images; p.27 (top) Courtesy Drexel University; p.27 (middle) Jean-Luc Lacour/NASA; p.27 (bottom) Javier Trueba/MSF/Science Photo Library; all other images from iStock and/or Shutterstock.

Library of Congress Cataloging-in-Publication Data

Names: Slepian, Curtis, author.
Title: Digging up dinosaurs / Curtis Slepian.
Description: Huntington Beach, CA : Teacher Created Materials, Inc., [2019] | Audience: Grade 4 to 6. | Includes index. |
Identifiers: LCCN 2018018107 (print) | LCCN 2018019832 (ebook) | ISBN 9781493869497 (E-book) | ISBN 9781493867097 (paperback)
Subjects: LCSH: Reptiles, Fossil--Juvenile literature. | Paleontology--Juvenile literature.
Classification: LCC QE861.5 (ebook) | LCC QE861.5 .S556 2019 (print) | DDC 560--dc23
LC record available at https://lccn.loc.gov/2018018107

Teacher Created Materials

5301 Oceanus Drive
Huntington Beach, CA 92649-1030
www.tcmpub.com
ISBN 978-1-4938-6709-7

Table of Contents

Prehistoric Wonders...4

Finding Fossils 6

Dig In! 10

At the Lab 16

Museum Monsters.. 21

More Cool Tools 27

STEAM Challenge... 28

Glossary 30

Index 31

Career Advice 32

Prehistoric Wonders

You are face-to-face with a mighty monster. It rises almost 4 meters (13 feet) above you and stretches about 12 meters (40 feet) long. A 1.5-m (5-ft.) long skull holds razor-sharp teeth as long as bananas! Luckily, this beast died about 66 million years ago. You are merely looking up at a **fossil** skeleton of a *Tyrannosaurus rex* (*T. rex*). It amazes thousands of visitors at a museum. The dinosaur fills you with wonder. It might also make you ask how this huge skeleton ended up here.

The road that fossils take to reach museums is hard and can take many years. It all starts with the work of **paleontologists**. Fossils help them learn about the prehistoric world. These scientists need a lot of skill and patience to locate fossils. To dig them up is hard, sweaty work. Then, bones must be cleaned and preserved. Experts at museums have to figure out how bones fit together. They use tools and technology to help get it all done. Some tools are as old-fashioned as a chisel and hammer, while others are as high-tech as **CT scanners**.

This T. rex, named Sue, was found by Sue Hendrickson near Faith, South Dakota.

The oldest fossils ever found are 4.2 billion-year-old bacteria discovered in rocks in Canada.

This 3-D rendering shows what a *T. rex* might have looked like when it was alive.

Finding Fossils

Fossils have been found on every continent—even in Antarctica. But how do people find them? Fossils are often found in **sedimentary rock**. This kind of rock is made of tiny bits of rock, gravel, and dust. Over millions of years, layers of **sediment** pile on top of one another. The sediment **compresses** and hardens. People can't see fossils on the ground in most places. The best places to look are arid, or dry, areas called badlands. There, **erosion** can expose fossils in the rocks. The dry western parts of the United States and Canada are places like this. They are magnets for fossil hunters.

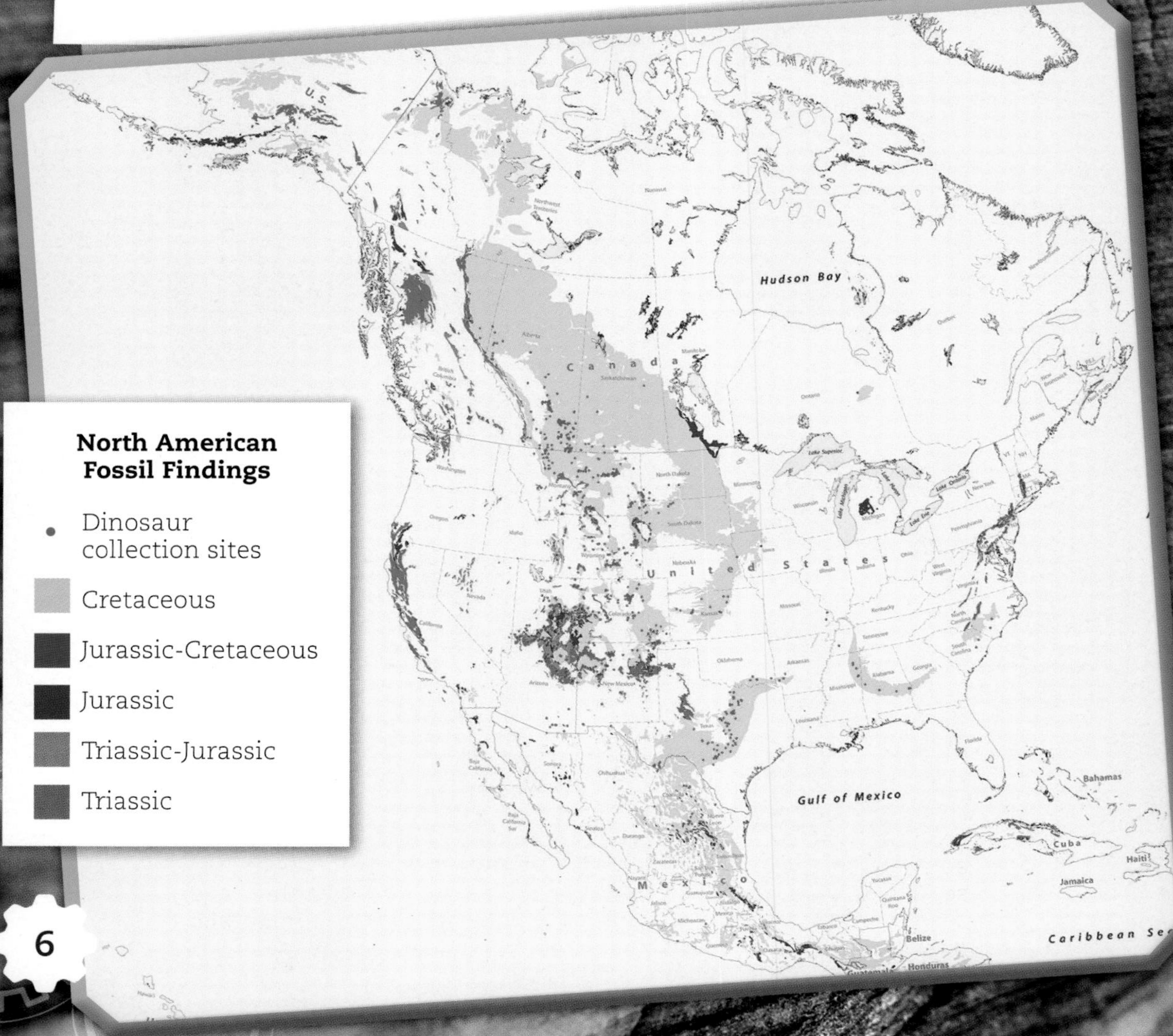

North American Fossil Findings
Dinosaur collection sites
Cretaceous
Jurassic-Cretaceous
Jurassic
Triassic-Jurassic
Triassic
U.S.
Hudson Bay
Canada
United States
Gulf of Mexico
Mexico
Bahamas
Cuba
Haiti
Jamaica
Belize
Honduras

What is the best way to find sedimentary rock and dry places? Scientists might first study a topographic map. This type of map shows the elevation of the ground and its features. Scientists check for places with little vegetation so fossils won't be hidden. A geological map also helps. This type of map shows the type of rock found on Earth's surface. Scientists search this type of map to find layers of sedimentary rock. If the rock was formed during the time of dinosaurs, it might hold the fossils they want.

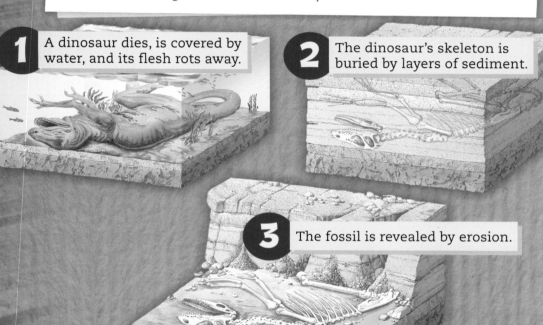

1 A dinosaur dies, is covered by water, and its flesh rots away.

2 The dinosaur's skeleton is buried by layers of sediment.

3 The fossil is revealed by erosion.

SCIENCE

Set in Stone

Most dinosaur fossils were formed when animals died near rivers or lakes and were quickly buried in mud, silt, or other sediments. Their flesh rotted away and left only hard parts, such as bones and teeth. Over thousands of years, layers of sediment piled over the bones. The pressure hardened the sediment into rock. Minerals in the rocks replaced the minerals in the remains of the animals. This process left fossils.

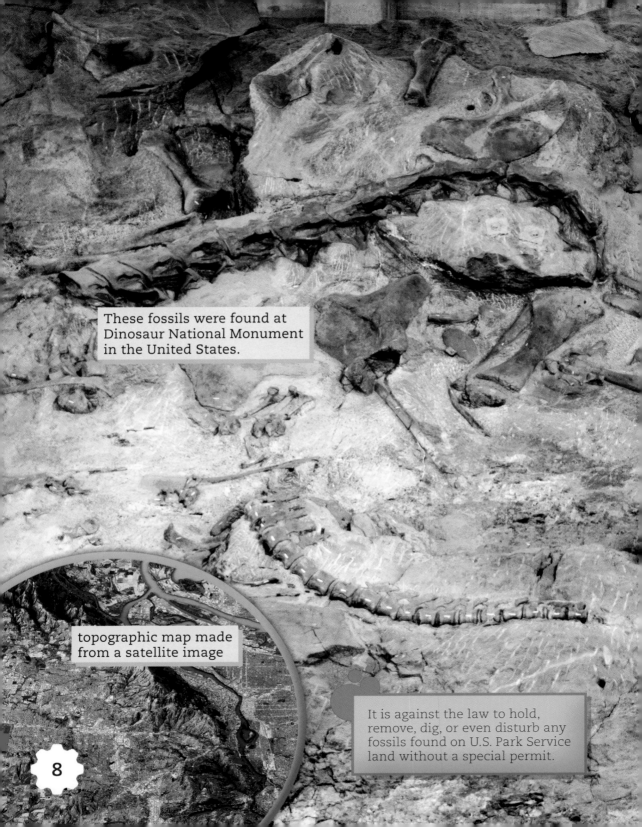

These fossils were found at Dinosaur National Monument in the United States.

topographic map made from a satellite image

It is against the law to hold, remove, dig, or even disturb any fossils found on U.S. Park Service land without a special permit.

A Closer Look

Sometimes, paleontologists have to search for fossils in remote places. They can be hundreds of kilometers wide. Fossil hunters do not want to hike for hours or days. Instead, they need to narrow the search area. One way to do so is by using satellite maps. NASA satellites orbit Earth. They take detailed images of Earth's surface. Scientists study the images. Then, they highlight areas of rock formations that might contain fossils.

Another way to look for fossils is to search where fossils have already been discovered. A team from Smithsonian's National Museum of Natural History has been doing just that. They are digging in one of North America's richest fossil sites. It is called the Hell Creek Formation. The area covers parts of Montana, Wyoming, and North and South Dakota. Hell Creek was formed about 66–70 million years ago. It was the time right before dinosaurs died off. For years, scientists have been digging ancient plant and animal fossils out of Hell Creek.

map of Hell Creek

A paleontologist digs fossils out of a pile of sedimentary rock.

9

Dig In!

Once they get to the right area, most paleontologists find fossils by prospecting. This involves walking around with their eyes focused on the ground. Scientists look for fossils sticking out of rock. They might spot bones or teeth scattered among rocks on the surface. This makes it important for scientists to be able to tell fossils from rocks. One way to tell is color. Fossils are often lighter or darker than surrounding rocks. Experts can also recognize bones by their shapes. Texture is another clue. Bones are often smoother and shinier than rocks.

Smithsonian paleontologists walk toward a hill in Hell Creek.

Scientists are more likely to find fossils in an area with **outcrops**, such as the sides of hills, cliffs, or dried-up riverbeds. Hell Creek has outcrops where wind and rain have exposed layers of rock. Fossil hunters check for bone fragments at the bottom of hills. Exposed fossils can fall out of rocks and roll downhill. By following trails of fragments up hills, paleontologists may be rewarded with exciting discoveries. Because ground can be rough and hilly, trucks are left behind. Paleontologists often hike for kilometers under a blazing sun before spotting a bone. Fossil hunts are tough work. But finding fossils makes the effort worthwhile.

Smithsonian scientists wrap plant fossils in toilet paper to safely transport them.

porous fossil

nonporous rock

Some paleontologists can identify fossils by licking them. A bone might stick slightly to the tongue because it is porous (having small holes), while a rock is not.

A scientist reads the patterns (right) from a ground-penetrating radar.

High-Tech Hunt

Not all fossils stick out of the ground. Most are hidden under the surface. Some paleontologists use high-tech tools to try to find these buried treasures. One device is ground-penetrating radar. In the field, a small radar device, which looks like a lawn mower, projects radio waves into the ground. The user reads the patterns that bounce back. As the user wheels the radar over the ground, patterns might change. A change in a pattern can indicate an object below.

Smithsonian paleontologists search for small bones at Hell Creek.

In the movie *Jurassic Park*, computer-assisted sonic tomography could show the outline of an entire dinosaur skeleton, but in real life it doesn't show that much detail.

Sound waves are another way to "see" under the ground. This technology is called computer-assisted sonic tomography. It works this way: People dig deep holes where fossils might be. Then, they hang special microphones into the holes. A person fires a slug, or bullet, at the ground in different areas. The microphones pick up the sounds of shock waves the slug makes. Experts determine whether the sound waves bounced off an object below. They can also guess how deep and large an object is. These devices are expensive and not always effective. So, most paleontologists search for fossils the old-fashioned way—by using their eyes and feet.

13

Rock On!

The Smithsonian team records the locations of every fossil they find with the aid of the Global Positioning System (GPS). A GPS device receives signals from navigation satellites. The signals locate where the holder stands to within about a meter (about a yard). But that's not accurate enough for a dig. Teams use two GPS devices that together pinpoint a location within a few centimeters (about half an inch). Teams also photograph fossils and sketch where they were found.

Then, the digging starts. Some fossils are buried in soft ground. Scientists uncover their upper surface with brushes and picks. But many fossils are trapped in hard rocks. It may take chisels, pickaxes, or even jackhammers to remove them. Paleontologists usually do not dig out just fossils. They also remove rocks around them. This secures the fossils. Team members gently chip away rock with sharp tools.

Finding and Preserving Fossils

1 Set up GPS device.

2 Record fossil location using GPS signals.

3 Dig out the fossil and surrounding rocks.

Next, paleontologists cover a bone and surrounding rock in a coat of plaster and burlap called a jacket. Some jacket-covered rocks are so heavy that a helicopter has to carry them away. The Smithsonian team once had to remove a one-ton jacket. Thinking fast, the team members turned a sheet of metal into a sled. They slid the jacket down a hill and into a truck. A jacket's next stop is a fossil laboratory.

Field journals like this help paleontologists record the locations of the fossils they find.

TECHNOLOGY

4

Cover the fossil in damp toilet paper and wrap it in a plaster jacket.

5

Flip the fossil to put the jacket at the bottom.

6

Tie jackets down for transport to the lab.

At the Lab

When jackets arrive at a fossil lab, **preparators** (prih-PEHR-uh-tuhrz) get ready to work. Their main job is to separate bones from rock. Throughout this process, preparators often view specimens through magnifying lenses or microscopes. First, they remove the jacket. Next, they use needles and air scribes. Air scribes are miniature jackhammers with small tips. They are the main tool preparators use to chip away rocks. When a rock is too hard, they use small grinding wheels or sand blasters. Then, more delicate tools come into play. Preparators use dental picks to dig out rocks from fossils' crevices. They use sewing needles to scrape away every last grain of stone. Lastly, they might treat the bones with special glues to keep them from falling apart.

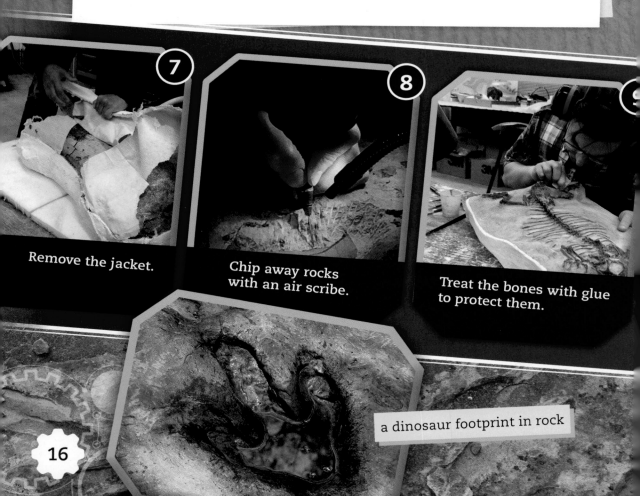

7

Remove the jacket.

8

Chip away rocks with an air scribe.

Treat the bones with glue to protect them.

a dinosaur footprint in rock

Preparators study field drawings and photos to learn where each bone fragment goes. This lets them perform precise work. And it helps them make sure fossils are not damaged in the cleaning process. Cleaned fossils are stored carefully. They need the right temperature and humidity. Big fossils might be placed in foam-covered plaster jackets. Smaller fossils go into special storage drawers. They all get numbers so they can be easily identified for later study. No wonder it can take years to prepare a large dinosaur fossil!

ENGINEERING

All Washed Up

Smithsonian preparators use a labor-saving invention that separates dirt from fossils. Two metal screens tied to either end of a string are loaded with sediment. The string is attached to a wheel. As the wheel turns, it lowers one screen into a bucket of water and lifts the other screen out of another bucket. It does this over and over until all dirt dissolves, leaving only fossils behind.

Smithsonian specialist Adam Metallo scans a whale fossil to create a 3-D image.

Smithsonian X 3D BETA

Tour: An Overview of Cerro Ballena

Step 1 of 11

A small fossil baleen whale, cataloged as MPC 684

Computer software creates a 3-D image of the scanned whale fossil.

3-D Bones

A museum might hold thousands of fossils in a storage area. These places are off-limits to the public. But researchers often come from all over the world to study the fossils up close. The problem is, fossils can be damaged when handled. Fortunately, researchers now can study dinosaur bones without touching them. They can use a CT scanner. Hospitals use this type of machine on people. But it works just as well on fossils. As it scans a bone, the machine rotates 360 degrees around it. It makes images of the fossil in thin slices. Computer software combines the slices to create a 3-D image of the fossil. The images even let scientists study the inside of bones without cutting them open. The digital files of the images can be emailed to scientists anywhere in the world.

Some scientists also use a special type of **laser** to produce 3-D pictures of fossils. These images show only the surface of objects. But the detail is even greater than that of a CT scan. Virtual fossils save scientists time and money. Scientists are able to study bones without having to see them in person. And museums can keep their fossils in good condition.

MATHEMATICS

Distinguishing Dinosaurs

Smithsonian's National Museum of Natural History has more than 40 million plant and animal fossils. Most fossils are kept in storage. So, the museum must use a cataloging system. Some systems are numerical starting with "1." Other systems use the dates that fossils were found with numbered details about where they were found. If someone wanted to see all the fossils, they would have to view more than 109,000 fossils every day for a year! That is 77 fossils per second!

Fossils can be big business. Sue the *T. rex* was sold to the Field Museum in Chicago for $8.36 million.

Museum Monsters

At a museum, complete dinosaur skeletons draw big crowds. But chances are that those fossils did not all come from the same dinosaur. Paleontologists often don't find complete skeletons, so museums fill in missing bones with fossils from different dinosaurs of the same type. Some fossils on display might not even be real. Many skeletons in museums are made partly of casts, or copies. There are a few reasons why a museum might make a cast of a fossil. Sometimes, there are no replacement fossils. Other times, fossils are too fragile or too heavy to display.

To create a cast, a preparator coats each side of a bone with silicon rubber. The flexible rubber makes an exact copy of the fossil's shape and texture. When the rubber dries, the worker can peel it off without damaging the bone. Then, the worker places the two rubber halves together to form a mold of the whole fossil. A material, such as resin, is poured into the mold through a small hole. When the material hardens, the worker peels off the rubber mold. Inside is a lightweight cast that is a nearly perfect copy of the bone. Lastly, a worker paints the cast to look like the real bone.

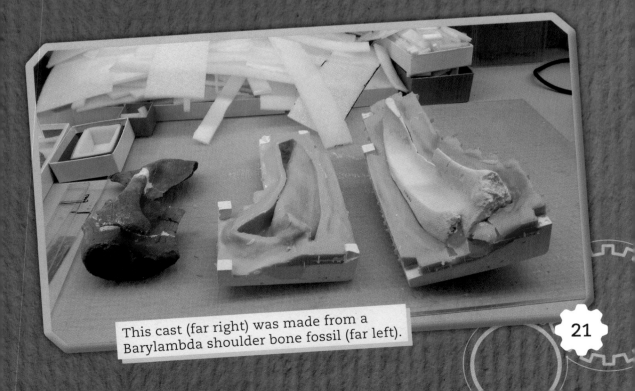

This cast (far right) was made from a Barylambda shoulder bone fossil (far left).

Raising *T. rex*

Smithsonian's newest dinosaur has a special nickname: the Nation's *T. rex*. It's also special because it is one of the world's largest, most complete *T. rex* skeletons. It has taken several years and many people to display it. Those people include scientists, welders, and engineers. Experts produced diagrams and small models of the dinosaur. These showed exactly where each bone should go. Vertical steel rods were built to carry most of the dinosaur's weight. Workers made a metal armature, or frame. The frame runs from the backbone through the tail. It was welded to the vertical rods. A blacksmith made more than a hundred individual brackets. These metal supports cradled the bones in the correct positions. Workers then attached the brackets to the frame. This is different from how it was done in the past. Museums used to drill holes in bones for the frames. This frame sits along the outside of the bones. It is not very noticeable to viewers. Any metal that touches the fossil is coated with special materials. They keep the metal from corroding or harming the bones.

The Nation's *T. rex* is posed as though it is eating another dinosaur. Scientists and workers made it look like it once was—one of the most ferocious animals to ever walk the earth.

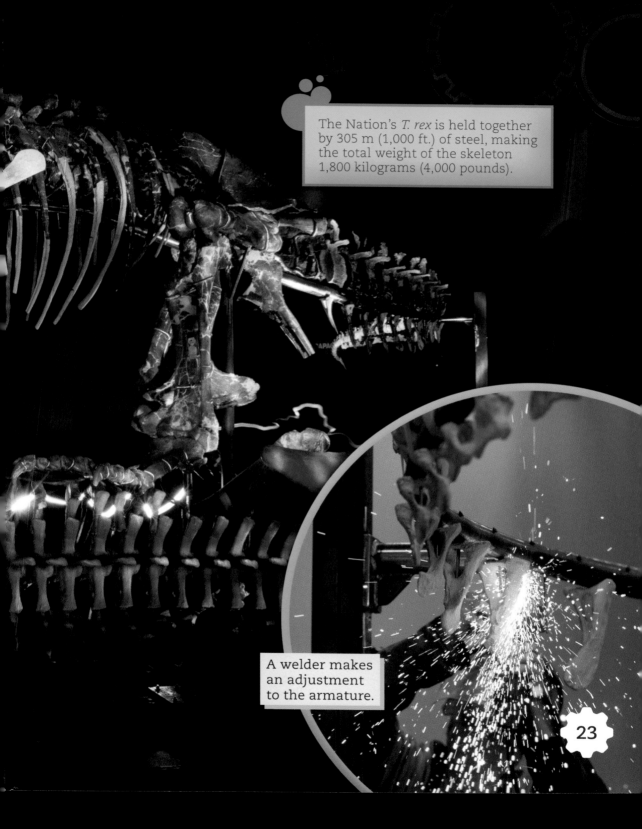

The Nation's *T. rex* is held together by 305 m (1,000 ft.) of steel, making the total weight of the skeleton 1,800 kilograms (4,000 pounds).

A welder makes an adjustment to the armature.

23

Fossil Fans

Many museums update their dinosaur halls as often as possible. Some add new dinosaurs. Others put dinosaurs they already have in different poses. They base the poses on new research that shows how dinosaurs stood and moved. For example, museums now display tyrannosaur skeletons with their tails off the ground. They also show the creatures stalking. This is more true to life. And it makes the dinosaurs look more exciting! But museums offer more than just fossils.

This crouched *Triceratops* skeleton is at Smithsonian's *The Last American Dinosaurs* exhibit in Washington, DC.

That is the case of *The Last American Dinosaurs* exhibit. It is in Smithsonian's National Museum of Natural History in Washington, DC. Here, visitors explore the ancient world of Hell Creek. A large painting imagines how it looked 66 million years ago. It shows a scene full of ancient plants and animals. There is a video game called "How to Become a Fossil." In it, players turn themselves into fossils. A video shows how scientists put together the exhibit. Another follows scientists on a fossil hunt. Guests can watch real people prepare fossils. Exhibits such as this one teach about dinosaurs in a hands-on way.

ARTS

Ancient Art

A mural at Smithsonian's National Museum of Natural History shows how Hell Creek might have looked when dinosaurs ruled it. Before painting the picture, paleoartist Mary Parrish studied the fossil collection at the museum. Parrish asked scientists how the animals behaved. She also studied similar animals that are alive today in a zoo, at a botanical garden, in the wild, and in books.

25

It is estimated that hundreds of millions (or even a few billion) of individual dinosaur fossils exist on the planet. But fewer than $\frac{1}{100}$ of them have been found so far.

More Cool Tools

New technology makes paleontologists' jobs easier. For example, scientists are now using **drones** to photograph fossil sites. Aerial photos help them see the whole landscape and spot bones more efficiently. Some drones even make 3-D photos or maps of sites. This is what happened in Africa. A science group used drones to photograph areas and then placed the images online. Anyone could search them to point out possible fossils. Their goal was to have people find fossils before they turned to dust.

Paleontologists also use 3-D printers. They turn computer files into solid objects. Scientists use these printers to make small models of bones and muscles. These help them learn how dinosaurs moved.

More amazing tools could be on the way. A laser on a NASA Mars rover has detected certain minerals on the Red Planet. One day, this technology might locate fossils on Earth. The laser would scan the ground. It would light up a certain chemical in bones. In museums, lighter, less visible materials could replace a skeleton's steel frame. Museums could do away with dinosaur bones. Instead, true-to-life dinosaur robots might give visitors the thrill of seeing these giant beasts move. These advances in technology will continue to produce even more clues about the past.

This 3-D model is of a *Dreadnoughtus* leg bone.

This computer-generated image shows a Mars rover with a laser.

A drone surveys a fossil site.

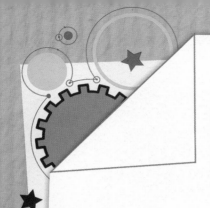

STEAM CHALLENGE

Define the Problem

You are a preparator for a natural history museum. The director of your dinosaur hall wants a new display for bones paleontologists have recently found. Your job is to create a model of a dinosaur that can be used as the model for the display.

Constraints: Your dinosaur model must be able to be viewed from all angles. Your model can be made from any materials (e.g., modeling clay, paper-mache, pipe cleaners, foil, etc.).

Criteria: Your dinosaur model must either have an armature to help it stand or be able to stand on its own.

Research and Brainstorm

What is the difference between a preparator and a paleontologist? What are the most important parts of a preparator's job? Why should a dinosaur be able to be viewed from all angles?

Design and Build

Sketch your dinosaur model. Will you have an armature or will it stand up on its own? What purpose will each part serve? What materials will work best? Build the model.

Test and Improve

Show your dinosaur model to a friend. Can they tell what type of dinosaur it is? Can your model stand up without falling over? How can you improve it? Modify your design and try again.

Reflect and Share

What other materials could you have used to make your model? How could you modify your display to make the dinosaur look like it was flying?

Glossary

compresses—squeezes or presses something so that it is smaller or fills less space

corroding—slowly breaking apart or being destroyed through a chemical process

CT scanners—X-ray machines that create 3-D images

drones—small aircraft guided by remote controls

erosion—the wearing away of something by water, wind, or glaciers

fossil—refers to the buried remains or traces of life from long ago, such as bone, shells, or footprints

fossil laboratory—a place where experts clean and preserve fossils

Global Positioning System (GPS)—a technology that pinpoints a location by sending signals from orbiting satellites to a receiver

jacket—a hard coating of plaster and cloth that protects fossils so they can be moved safely

jackhammers—large power tools used to break hard rock or other materials

laser—a concentrated, powerful beam of light

outcrops—the parts of rock formations that stick out of the ground

paleontologists—scientists who study fossils to understand the prehistoric world

preparators—skilled experts who clean and preserve fossils in laboratories

radar—a system that sends radio waves to detect and locate objects

resin—a sticky material that can be used to cover and protect

sediment—a layer of stones, sand, mud, shells, or other very small pieces of matter

sedimentary rock—rock made of rock grains deposited by wind or water

slug—a type of bullet

Index

Canada, 5–6

casts, 21

Chicago, 20

CT scanners, 4, 19

Field Museum, 20

Global Positioning System (GPS), 14

Hell Creek Formation, 9–11, 13, 25

Jurassic Park, 13

Last American Dinosaurs, The, exhibit, 24–25

Montana, 9

NASA, 9, 27

National Museum of Natural History, 9, 19, 25

Nation's *T. rex*, 22–23

North America, 6, 9

North Dakota, 9

paleontologists, 4, 9–15, 21, 27

Parrish, Mary, 25

preparators, 16–17, 21

South Dakota, 5, 9

Tyrannosaurus rex (*T. rex*), 4–5, 20, 22–23

Washington, DC, 24–25

Wyoming, 9

CAREER ADVICE
from Smithsonian

Do you want to work with fossils?
Here are some tips to get you started.

"Being a paleontologist is a dream come true. You find and study the remains of animals and plants that lived unimaginably long ago. The search for fossils can take you anywhere – close to home or to remote regions of the globe."
— *Hans-Dieter Sues, Paleontologist* **(shown right)**

"Fossils are amazing and the best ones are still waiting to be discovered. I started finding fossils when I was 5 years old and you can too. Learn how to look by reading books and visiting museums. Then convince your parents to take you to places where you can start looking." —*Kirk Johnson, Sant Director, National Museum of Natural History* **(shown left)**